The Downtown Ducks

Third Printing

By

Richard Alex Repp

Illustrations
By
Richard Alex Repp
Mary L. Repp
Anya K. Repp

The Downtown Ducks

This book is dedicated to my children, Alex and Anya, my nephews, Kaden, James, Walter, and Benjamin, my niece Kaileigh, and all their cousins, with special gratitude to my parents, Rod and Mary, who always encouraged me to draw and pursue my dreams, and to my wife, Lisa, who has supported all my various activities.
I love you all.
(Happy Birthday, Mom!)

Author: Richard A. Repp
PO Box 21142, Spokane, WA 99201
TheDowntownDucks2023@gmail.com

Publisher: Sunshine Idaho Publishing, LLC
PO Box 2714, Hayden, ID 83835
SunshineIdaho208@outlook.com

ISBN 979-8-9898595-2-8

The Downtown Ducks

One day, a duck began to build a nest.

She flew far and wide, gathering sticks for the nest.

After building the nest, she laid some eggs.

The duck had built her nest high in a planter, outside the office window of a banker named Joel.

Joel and his co-workers enjoyed watching the nesting duck.

After about 30 days, ten little ducklings hatched. But how were the baby ducklings going to get down to their mother?

Joel ran down to the sidewalk below to catch
the ducklings as they began to jump off the ledge.

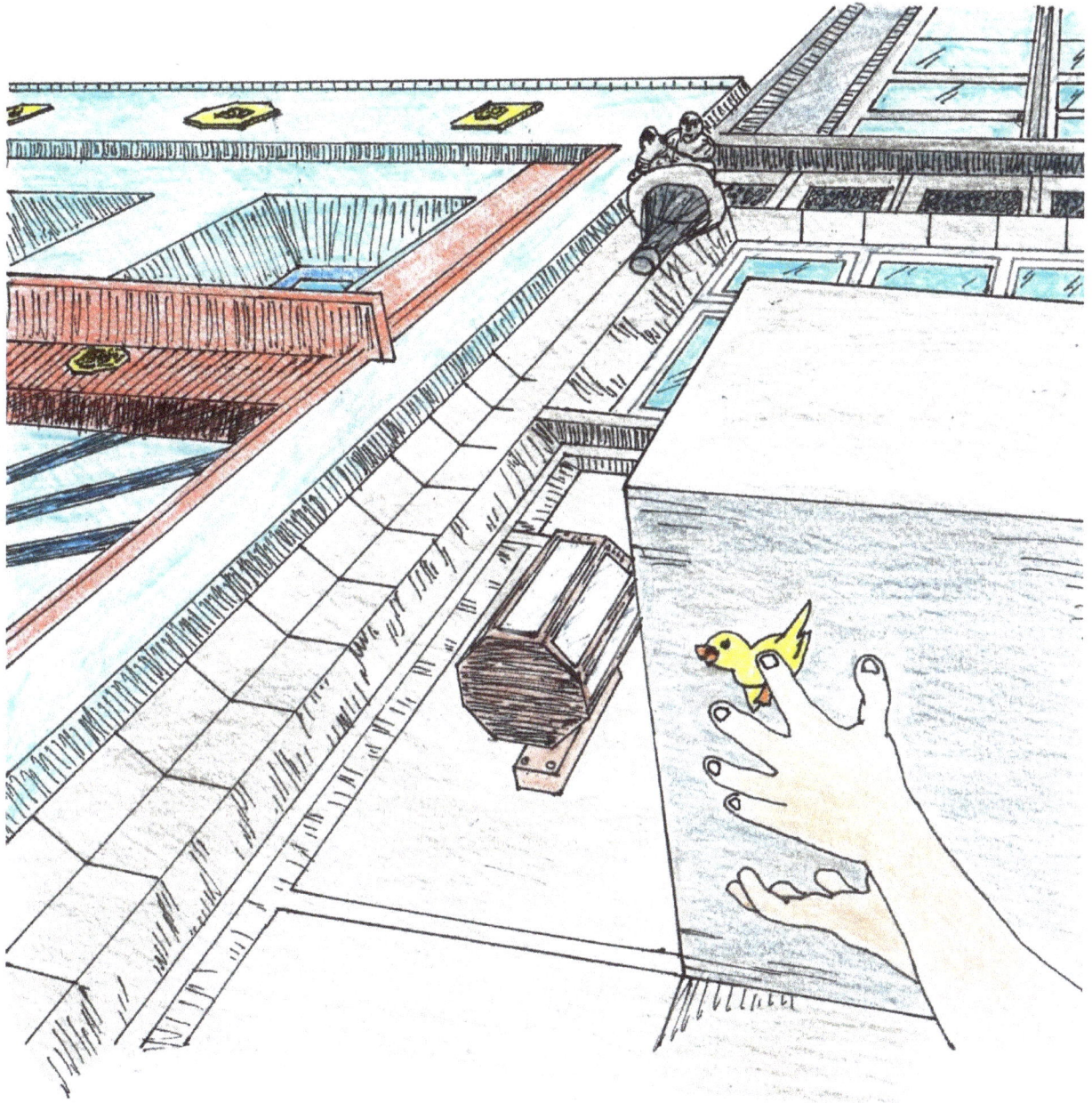

One by one, Joel placed the ducklings in a box.

The mother duck seemed to know that Joel was helping her and her ducklings.

The mother duck followed Joel and the ducklings through downtown, towards the river, even past a parade.

At the river, Joel let the ducklings out of the box so they could follow their mother to the water.

The mother and her ducklings made their own parade
as they ran towards the river.

Joel cheered the ducklings as they ran.

One by one, they jumped into the water.

Safely in the water, the mother duck and all the ducklings swam away, quacking, as if to say "thank you" to Joel and his friends.

The end.

About this Story:

"The Downtown Ducks" is based on the true story of Joel Armstrong,
a banker with Sterling Savings Bank in downtown Spokane, Washington
who observed the ducks outside his office window and helped them
reach the Spokane River, a couple of blocks away.

THE SPOKESMAN-REVIEW

'Duck guy' looks back on memorable year

December 27, 2008 - By Meghann M. Cuniff - Photo by Jesse Tinsley

Joel Armstrong looks out his window at Sterling Savings on Wednesday at the first-floor awning where ducks nested earlier in the year. Armstrong watched the ducks, nest, lay eggs and then hatch them. After seeing one duckling fall to the ground, he caught the rest of them as they fell and carried them to the river.

To read the full article, go to:

https://www.spokesman.com/stories/2008/dec/27/duck-guy-looks-back-memorable-year/

THE SPOKESMAN-REVIEW

Ducks make a splash with parade of their own

May 17, 2009 - By Jody Lawrence-Turner - Photo by Jesse Tinsley

It took a troupe of bank employees and a phalanx of bystanders and media, but eventually a hen duck and 12 ducklings slid into the water in Riverfront Park Saturday.

To read the full article, go to:

https://www.spokesman.com/stories/2009/may/17/ducks-make-a-splash-with-parade-of=their-own

Television Coverage

YouTube:

ABC News Channel - Good Morning America (2008)

"Banker Saves a Dozen Ducklings From Ledge"
https://www.youtube.com/watch?v=VAqWC3Cpny8

ABC News Channel - World News Webcast (2009)

"Spokane's Duck Man"
https://www.youtube.com/watch?v=0SGIYiU8bZM

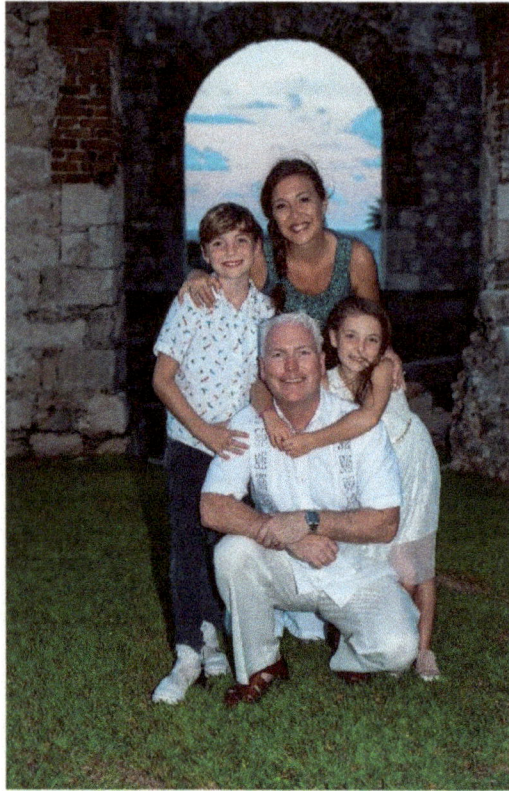

About the Author

Richard Alex Repp, known by friends and family as "Rick", grew up wanting to be a cartoonist and then an architect. He was accepted to the Cornell College of Architecture with an application portfolio that consisted mostly of cartoons. He is now a corporate attorney working in an office building adjacent to the historic Cutter Tower where the ducklings hatched. No ducks have built a nest outside his window yet, but he keeps hoping.

About the Illustrations:

Rick's mother, Mary L. (Anderson) Repp was a dedicated homemaker and farmwife during his upbringing, and her talented amateur paintings and artwork with a variety of mediums, inspired and encouraged Rick's own love of art. She and Rick's daughter, Anya, helped color the illustrations drawn by Rick.

www.ingramcontent.com/pod-product-compliance
Lightning Source LLC
Chambersburg PA
CBHW041604260326
41914CB00011B/1380